Dec 18

Building Character

# Showing Kindness

by Rebecca Pettiford

Bullfrog Books

# Ideas for Parents and Teachers

Bullfrog Books let children practice reading informational text at the earliest reading levels. Repetition, familiar words, and photo labels support early readers.

## Before Reading
- Discuss the cover photo. What does it tell them?

- Look at the picture glossary together. Read and discuss the words.

## Read the Book
- "Walk" through the book and look at the photos. Let the child ask questions. Point out the photo labels.

- Read the book to the child, or have him or her read independently.

## After Reading
- Prompt the child to think more. Ask: How do you show kindness? How does it make you feel when you are kind?

Bullfrog Books are published by Jump!
5357 Penn Avenue South
Minneapolis, MN 55419
www.jumplibrary.com

Library of Congress Cataloging-in-Publication Data

Names: Pettiford, Rebecca, author.
Title: Showing kindness / by Rebecca Pettiford.
Description: Bullfrog Books.
Minneapolis, Minnesota: Jump!, Inc., [2018]
Series: Building character | Audience: K to Grade 3.
Audience: Age: 5–8.| Includes index.
Identifiers: LCCN 2017029251 (print)
LCCN 2017031221 (ebook)
ISBN 9781624966477 (ebook)
ISBN 9781620318867 (hardcover: alk. paper)
ISBN 9781620318874 (pbk.)
Subjects: LCSH: Kindness—Juvenile literature.
Classification: LCC BJ1533.K5 (ebook)
LCC BJ1533.K5 P448 2017 (print) | DDC 177/.7—dc23
LC record available at https://lccn.loc.gov/2017029251

Editor: Kirsten Chang
Book Designer: Michelle Sonnek
Photo Researchers: Michelle Sonnek & Kirsten Chang

Photo Credits: Brian Chase/Shutterstock, cover; wavebreakmedia/Shutterstock, 1, 4, 5, 23tl; marekuliasz/Shutterstock, 3; Picture-Factory/Adobe Stock, 6–7; racorn/Shutterstock, 8; rukxstockphoto/Shutterstock, 9; Jose Luis Pelaez Inc/Alamy, 10–11; Bloomicon/Shutterstock, 12 (girl), 23bl; Pe3k/Shutterstock, 12 (Earth), 23bl; njgphoto/iStock, 13 (bin), 23tr; mphillips007/iStock, 13 (trash), 23tr; wong sze yuen/Shutterstock, 14–15; Cherednychenko Ihor/Shutterstock, 16–17; EvgeniiAnd/Shutterstock, 18–19; Comstock Images/Getty, 20–21; Prostock-studio/Shutterstock, 22 (top); Nattika/Shutterstock, 22 (bottom); Vixit/Shutterstock, 23br (foreground); Evgeny Karandaev/Shutterstock, 23br (background); VaLiza/Shutterstock, 24 (boy); Beth Swanson/Shutterstock, 24 (chalk).

Printed in the United States of America at Corporate Graphics in North Mankato, Minnesota.

## Table of Contents

# True Kindness

We like showing kindness.

We show kindness
by doing good deeds.

We make others happy.

5

Sami is new in school.

Nan is kind to him.

She smiles. She sits with him at lunch.

Now they are friends.

Jon lost his pencil.

8

Beth kindly gives him one.
Now he can take his test.

Drew is kind
to his mom.

He helps her put
groceries away.

# Ruth is kind to the planet.

planet

She recycles.

Recycling is good for the planet.

Ryan is kind to his sister.

He plays with her.

He shares his toys.

Pete is kind to his cat.

He pets her softly.

Max is sad.

Ann is kind to him.

She listens.

It helps him
feel better.

It feels good to be kind!

# Acts of Kindness

**Practice acts of kindness by making a Kindness Board.**

## You will need:

- a sheet of paper
- a pencil
- a ruler
- crayons or colored pencils

## Directions:

❶ Use your ruler to draw straight lines. Draw 9 boxes on your "board" like the one on this page.

❷ Write an act of kindness in each box. Use the acts of kindness in the example above, or use others from this book. You can also make up your own.

❸ After you do an act of kindness, color inside the box. See how many acts of kindness you can do in a day!

### Kindness Board

| Hold a door open for someone | Help someone with a chore | Play with a brother or sister |
|---|---|---|
| Say "hello" to someone new | Give someone a compliment | Brush your dog or cat |
| Say "please" and "thank you" | Eat lunch with someone new | Write a letter to a friend |

# Picture Glossary

**deeds**
Actions or things that someone does.

**recycles**
Sends paper, bottles, and cans to a place where they are made into something new.

**planet**
A large, round object in space that travels around a star like the sun. Earth is a planet.

**test**
A set of questions or problems that measure knowledge or what you know.

# Index

# To Learn More

Learning more is as easy as 1, 2, 3.

1) Go to www.factsurfer.com

2) Enter "showingkindness" into the search box.

3) Click the "Surf" button to see a list of websites.

With factsurfer.com, finding more information is just a click away.